When I look at myself in the mirror, I see a unicorn.

A BADASS UNICORN.

THE
WISDOM
OF
UNICORNS

JOULES TAYLOR

ILLUSTRATIONS BY DANIELLE NOEL

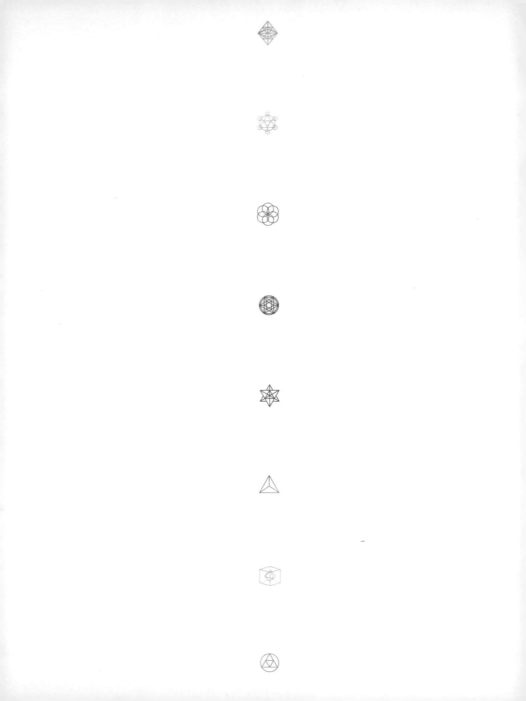

CONTENTS

UNICORNS
EXIST

You may not be able to find one in your local park, but unicorns are just as real as the qualities they embody.

Joy.
Strength.
Well-being.

The unicorn is the perfect spiritual guardian. And who doesn't need a little spiritual guidance, now and then?

Discovering our personal unicorn and channelling its awesome positive power – whether through dreams, meditation or serendipity – provides an unlimited source of advice and guidance whenever we need it most.

Our unicorns have our backs. Their strength can be our strength. Their courage and wisdom ours, too, when we have difficult decisions to make or challenges to overcome.

Unicorns are our most sympathetic listeners – they're not here to judge. They are our cheerleaders, ready to remind us of our own power when we need it most and to lend us their purity of purpose when the going gets tough.

We turn to our unicorns for any number of reasons. Maybe we need a little bit of self-care. Maybe we're feeling stressed at work or at home. Or maybe we're ready to make changes in our lives, our careers or our relationships, and we want that extra little bit of extra guidance to help show us the way.

Connecting with our unicorns helps us
connect with ourselves. And it teaches us to
trust our own instincts and our strengths.

Our unicorns make our lives and the world
an infinitely better, more magical place.

And yours is waiting for you –
you just have to look inside yourself to
find it. This book will show you how.
So go on! What are you waiting for?
Go and find your unicorn.

They said
I could
be anything,
so I
became a
UNIC<u>O</u>RN.

WHY WE NEED UNICORNS

Imagine climbing a hill on a clear day.

When you look around, you can see your world spread
out before you, feel your path firm beneath your feet.
The air you breathe is as crystalline as the view.

Now imagine carrying that sense of clarity and freedom inside
you, all day, every day. Imagine how amazing that would feel.

But what if you don't live on an idyllic hilltop in a beautiful
sylvan setting? Because, I'll be honest, not many of us do.

What if your life is a little more like the rest of ours?
Busy, stressful and sometimes maybe even a little chaotic?

Well, that's where our unicorns come in.

———

Your unicorn is a creature of pure energy. It is not earthbound, as we are, but exists in a higher dimension. Which means its point of view is crystal clear. Past, present, future – all are spread out beneath its benevolent gaze. It has the kind of perspective we know we need, but which can seem almost impossibly out of reach when we're caught up in the day-to-day struggles of a world that can be crude, stressful and even cruel.

But our unicorns see the way clearly. Our unicorns know our deepest wishes and desires and, like true friends, they will us onwards to our goals. They watch us when we stumble – and we all stumble – and they accept us, flaws and all. If we let them, they gently pick us back up again, show us where we went wrong and help us avoid making the same mistake twice. And, as they do, they teach us to forgive ourselves, as they forgive us.

———

I am stronger than this challenge. AND THIS CHALLENGE IS MAKING ME STRONGER.

The unicorn's nature is not the same as ours. It's untamed, less rule-bound, wilder and more instinctive. Unicorns enjoy absolute freedom. And, if we allow them to, they wish to share this with us.

Unicorns teach us how to love ourselves and others freely, in a pure and unselfish way. They love us for what we are, not what we can give or do, and they show us how to do the same. They teach us how to care more for others, to be kinder and more considerate, to make things better.

And over and above their concern for us, unicorns are the guardians of the natural world, and can teach us how to love and nurture our planet. And that, my friend, is good for *all* of us!

WHAT IS
A UNICORN?

Seems like a simple question, doesn't it? A unicorn is a
fabulous, mythical beast. A wild, white horse with a single
spiral horn growing from the middle of its forehead.
Sometimes it has wings. It always has healing powers.

So far, so familiar. And yet, for a creature so beloved around
the world, there is surprisingly little we can point to in our
quest to learn what, exactly, a unicorn is.

This is perhaps because the unicorn's secretive nature means it was traditionally only found in the wildest and most difficult-to-reach places. Ancient fables describe them in the Himalayan mountains, the dense jungles of South America and India, the swamps of North America, the ancient forests and mountain ranges of Europe, under the ice of the Arctic.

Equally likely, however, is that the scarcity of accounts is because although unicorns are *in* the world, they are not really *of* it. They are beings of pure energy, who exist on a different plane from our physical world. Only under the right circumstances can we be aware of them – just like we are aware of the wind, or heat, or cold, even though we can't see these things with the unaided eye.

*'Life is the wind
and the rain and the
thunder in the sky ...
what is and what is not,
and what beyond
is in Eternity.'*

Seneca

And yet despite unicorns' elusive nature, travellers' tales, songs and poems through the ages are full of tantalizing snippets of unicorn lore. Across the globe, legends persist – whether in tales of Noah's ark, stories of King Arthur's knights or myths of the Japanese *kirin*, a deer-like creature with a long flowing mane and a voice that sounds like wind chimes.

Several less exalted historical accounts also exist, variously identifying narwhals, prehistoric aurochs, oryx and even rhinoceroses as unicorns. But none of these rather prosaic horned animals can really explain the enduring hold the unicorn has on the human imagination.

Most compelling is a consistent belief that unicorns are spirit guides, otherworldly beings given to us as guardians and helpers before we are born. They are protective: they act to guide us and warn us if we're about to do something that could harm us. However, they have to be asked to take action, to contact us. They will never barge in and take over. We need to invite them into our lives.

And to do that, we need to know not only *how* to ask, but *what* to ask. What qualities do we wish to invoke in our unicorns and ourselves? Only once we have these firmly at the heart of our pursuit can we begin to summon our own personal unicorn – and to embrace the power that entails.

'Well, now that we *have* seen each other,' said the unicorn, 'if you believe in me, I'll believe in you.'

Lewis Carroll, *Through the Looking Glass*

QUALITIES OF
A UNICORN

HEALING POWERS

Unicorns are healers.

This is perhaps their most commonly known property.
A unicorn's horn, its touch, its breath, its very being as a whole
have healing properties that have been noted for centuries.

According to Arthurian legend, when Sir Elad of Salisbury
was being driven mad by sorrow, the breath of a unicorn
restored him to health and sanity. Further legend has it
that the unicorn's horn cleanses water of all poisons.

———————

Today, most of the unicorn's healing is of the
spiritual and mental kind. After all, we now have
highly skilled doctors to tend to most of our physical
ills, but sometimes our counsellors need a little help
in dealing with our less obvious problems.

Which is not surprising, given that it is not always
easy to recognise a need to heal in ourselves.
But once we are able to identify our own need,
we can call on our unicorn to help.

You might find a daily affirmation helpful in
focusing your energies on this most potent
aspect of your unicorn's power.

———————

I am confident *in all that I do.*

I stand up for myself.

I respect *myself at all times.*

I choose health, healing and happiness.

I act with courage and strength.

I deserve a wonderful *life.*

I will seek the divine
in every situation.

*I will look beyond the
surface to find the* light
in every person.

*I will seek to be aware of
the* wonder *of creation.*

*I will delight in
everything, for joy is the
key to* enlightenment.

JOY

Your unicorn is joyful.

It's said that unicorns have higher and more refined senses than any other creature – that they can actually smell and hear joy and love. They hear music in all things, even in sunlight and starlight, raindrops, plants growing, butterflies flitting among flowers and especially happy human thoughts. They are drawn to beauty and joyful things, and some can sing, a rare and glorious sound.

According to one legend, at the time of the Biblical flood, as the other animals boarded Noah's Ark, the unicorns were so light of spirit, so joyous in nature, that they simply couldn't believe harm might come to them and stayed frolicking on the hillsides until it was too late to join the other animals.

Your unicorn wants to bring you joy and to share its capacity for delight with you. Practise opening yourself to happiness to summon and celebrate this aspect of your unicorn's character.

WISDOM

Your unicorn is wise.

The unicorn's power, strength and wisdom come from
deep within the creature. Its sagacity has long been
recognized in cultures all over the world. The Chinese
qilin is one possible form a unicorn can take. It usually
appears when something significant is about to happen,
such as the birth of someone very important, and is
always a good omen. It often has the head of a lion and a
powerful body covered in scales. In Chinese mythology,
the *qilin* is one of the four intelligent animals, the others
being the phoenix, the tortoise and the dragon.

Your unicorn's wisdom is one of the most precious gifts
it can bestow. But you must be ready to receive it and
willing to embrace the gentle guidance it can provide.

Wisdom *is*
awakened in me.

I listen to the
knowledge in my heart.

I have all the wisdom I need
to experience my highest good
with ease *and* grace.

I move forward
with courage.

I am safe *and* secure.

*I breathe out
anxiety and
breathe in* calm.

*As my world expands,
so do my* heart
and mind.

LOYALTY

Your unicorn's devotion is limitless.

The unicorn is the brave, loyal defender of the
innocent, especially of those who love the earth
and the life our planet supports.

Yet the unicorn is a paradox – it is as gentle as baby
and as fierce as a warrior! It sees and understands
the magic, the possibilities, within the human spirit
that calls to it, and it is always ready to respond.

FREEDOM

Your unicorn cannot be tamed.

The unicorn is excellent at hiding itself away from
hunters or anyone wishing to capture it or do it harm.
In Medieval times, it was said that only a virgin maiden
could calm a unicorn: if she were to sit under a tree in a
forest the unicorn would come to her and lay its head in
her lap, and then it could be captured – or become her
guardian. With the innocent and pure of heart it was
gentle and loving, protective and caring. If captured
and imprisoned, though, it would pine away.

Embrace and welcome your unicorn's
strength and liberty.

LIVE
LIKE
SOMEONE
LEFT
THE
GATE
OPEN.

NOBLE PROTECTOR – LOYAL FRIEND

The single most unique thing about the unicorn is that it
is so very unlike the other beasts of legend, who often prey
on humans. The unicorn has *always* been a protector and
guardian. This is a noble, innocent creature, and an intensely
loyal friend to humans who love it. Yes, the unicorn is not
a *tame* creature, and can be very dangerous when its protective
instincts are roused, but normally it is a shy, gentle and loving
beast, guarding the planet and the living things on it,
and its chosen human most of all.

Silence
isn't empty.

It's full of
answers.

WHERE IS YOUR UNICORN?

The modern world can sometimes seem determined to reject magic. And yet, myths and mythical creatures are everywhere – in fiction, songs and poetry, and illustrated in greetings cards, doodles and even street art. In fact, there have never been so many unicorns around. And yours is here, too – you just have to know where to look.

Everything worthwhile takes a little effort. Only by taking a step back from your everyday, busy, noisy and chaotic life, to be quiet and focus on yourself and your inner needs, will you be able to find your unicorn. In stillness, it will come to you, this beautiful, powerful protector, to enrich your life. You only need to listen.

HOW TO CHANNEL
YOUR UNICORN

There's a unicorn out there for everyone.

Your own personal cosmic creature is waiting for you, but
how do you find it? What is the secret to connecting to
your spirit guide, who will stay close to you throughout
your life, and who will help you whenever you call them?

It's easy to channel your very own awe-inspiring and
magical guardian – all it takes is a little discipline and
an open mind. Here are some techniques to help
summon your unicorn to you.

DREAMS

The unicorn is a creature of the night-time, strongly associated with moonlight and starlight. Unsurprisingly, therefore, it often comes to us in our dreams. Or it may make contact with you most easily when you're drowsy, between the waking and sleeping worlds.

After all, unicorns are real to us in much the same way dreams are. Dreams, like unicorns, aren't tangible, and yet they inspire art, music, even scientific discoveries. Without dreaming, we simply can't function – we become stressed and irritable, we're unable to concentrate and our blood pressure rises.

Going through life without our unicorns at our side can have the same effect. Conversely, meeting our unicorns can help to reduce our stress levels, calm our over-busy minds and give us a deep sense of calm and comfort.

Dreaming of unicorns, and connecting with them when awake, is said to bring us strength, honesty and purity of purpose.

PREPARING YOUR DREAM QUEST

Before you go to sleep, bring yourself into a state of open-mindedness and relaxation. Sometimes it helps if you set yourself a routine to create a calm and welcoming atmosphere. Your environment should be as gentle as your intention. Some of the rituals below might help.

Eat a light snack – fruit is great – shower or bathe, and wear something loose and comfortable.

Play music – soft and dreamy is usually best.

Turn down the lights or maybe light a candle or two to provide a soft glow.

Sit somewhere comfortable for a few minutes and focus on this single thought:

'Tonight, I will meet my unicorn!'

Prepare for sleep with this thought at the forefront of your mind.

It can take time, so don't worry if it doesn't work right away. Try to spend at least five minutes doing this before going to bed, but the longer the better, as this will fix the idea more firmly in your mind and make it easier for your unicorn to find you. Stay positive, and keep trying!

And keep an open mind. Remember that when your unicorn first appears to you out of your sleepy haze, it may initially be merely as a sound or a name, or you might catch sight of a wisp of mane or the shadow of a horn. These are all excellent signs that your unicorn is near and trying to reveal itself to you!

You must learn
a new way to

THINK

before you
can learn a new
way to

BE.

Once you have met your unicorn for the first time, it will be easier to meet it again. The next time you prepare for a dream quest, try to remember the sound or name or the vision you experienced in your first encounter, and focus on it next time you fall asleep to call your unicorn to you. Again, focus on this thought:

'Tonight, I will meet my unicorn!'

It takes a lot of practice, but it's quite possible to learn lucid dreaming – the power to change and shape your own dreams – so that you can summon your unicorn at will. Being able to choose to meet your unicorn in dreams is a wonderful experience.

Keep a dream diary by your bed and write down
everything you remember about your encounter as soon
as you're awake enough to use a pen. After a while,
you'll be able to remember more and more.

The next step is to tell yourself, every night:

'I can control my dreams.'

Very soon you will, and you can call your unicorn
to join you whenever you want.

MEDITATION

Meditation is simply focusing on something in order to gain a positive result. Many of us do it without even realising it! When we lose ourselves watching clouds, for instance, or gazing out over a beautiful view. We meditate unconsciously when we feel our minds unfurl as we walk by the sea, listen to a favourite piece of music or simply enjoy *being* somewhere, soaking up the beauty of a place without worrying about anything else.

Meditation like this is vital for our well-being. Not only is it very healthy for mind, body and spirit, but it can help you connect with your unicorn! And anyone can do it, any time, anywhere.

'I think 99 times
and I find nothing.

I stop thinking,
swim in silence,
and the truth
comes to me.'

Albert Einstein

CLEAR YOUR MIND

This is easier said than done! The human mind is
eternally curious and busy. But each time you achieve
a state of relaxation, and realise how good it feels, you
will find it easier to do next time. Even when your
mind starts buzzing again, you'll feel more rested,
and ready to enjoy your unicorn's company.

The following tips can help.

QUIET

Take a minute to turn your attention inwards and listen to
what's going on in your head. Are stray thoughts bubbling up
from nowhere? You may find yourself humming snippets of
a song or three you particularly like, or making a mental list
of what you need to do later. There's those things you need to
buy, what you're going to wear tomorrow, that card you need to
remember for your friend's birthday, oh, and you keep forgetting
to call that person you said you'd speak to later . . .

The noise and clutter can be quite overwhelming, and it can be
difficult to bring it all under control. But the unicorn is a calm
beast, and it will reward your efforts to still your mind! It will
bring its own deep and wonderful serenity to add to yours.

MANTRAS

Start simple, and don't expect to get it right first time! One
very old and trusted way to calm your mind is to choose a
word or phrase as a mantra. Traditionally, the Hindu and
Buddhist sacred sound '*om*' was used to focus the mind, but it's
not necessary to use that. Your mantra could be your unicorn's
name, if you know it, or a word that suggests stillness or
tranquility – 'space', 'ocean' or 'peace' perhaps. Say the word
over and over again, slowly, either in your mind or aloud,
until it's all you can hear.

I am calm
and focused *now.*

My unicorn is with me.
I am safe *and* protected.

I am fully present
in the moment.

The universe *gives me* everything *I need.*

I have complete health *now.*

I am deeply loved.

VISIONS

If you've chosen a mantra that conjures up an image – some soft clouds or gentle waves – you may find that this vision naturally fills your mind. Allow it. Your vision may begin to transform into the shape of your unicorn.

Alternatively, you can choose a more familiar, comforting image. It could be as simple as a steaming cup of coffee or rain on a windowpane, or something more complex like a favourite picture. Concentrate on the image until it's all you can think about.

PLACE

Perhaps the best and easiest way to meet your unicorn is to sit
quietly and imagine a favourite place. This can be anywhere.
A good starting point might be to envision those wild,
difficult-to-reach places where unicorns were traditionally
found. Maybe a forest, a seashore, a clifftop, a meadow;
in shallow coral seas or by frozen pools in icy mountains.

But it doesn't need to be anywhere exotic: your own
room, a library, the swimming pool or your favourite
park are all perfectly fine settings.

Or imagine yourself floating in space, absolutely still and
silent, basking in gentle sun- or starlight. Focus on the
emptiness around you, deep and restful, with just the bright
glittering of distant stars to contrast the deep black of the void.

Whichever place works for you, your unicorn will not
refuse the location you suggest – it wants to come to you.
Imagine yourself in that favourite place, eager to meet
your unicorn, and it will appear.

CRYSTALS

Some people find that gazing into a crystal is a good way to calm the mind. Look into the crystal: if it's a transparent stone, see if it contains any marks, veins, shapes or rainbows. Look deeply enough and you will see that crystal interiors can look like light-filled caverns, mazes, cliffs and spires. Try imagining yourself inside it, exploring your crystal's inner landscape. Later, when you're ready, you might like to explore it all again, with your unicorn beside you.

BREATHE

Focus on your breathing. Feel yourself pulling air into your lungs, holding it for a few seconds, then breathing out, slowly and steadily. As you breathe out, imagine yourself as light, free and wild as your unicorn. This not only helps you relax and clear your mind, but is also good for your body's health.

Now your mind is clear and still, and you're ready to
summon your unicorn. If you have already encountered your
unicorn in your dreams, return your thoughts to the place
where you first met. Imagine it in as much detail as you can.

When you're ready, invite your unicorn to join you –
if it's not already there waiting for you!

HOW TO SPOT
YOUR UNICORN

Sometimes your unicorn is so keen to join you it will arrive
all of a sudden, often when you least expect it! It can happen
anywhere – walking along a street, shopping, reading, eating –
but usually when you're alone or feeling lonely. You'll
suddenly feel an airy presence just behind you. You'll feel safe
and protected, as if a strong friend is guarding your back. If
you are very lucky, you may see, out of the corner of your eye,
the faint shimmery outline of a horn or a star-filled unicorn's
eye. Think 'Welcome!' and greet your new guardian.

———

A sudden feeling of comfort, contentment or joy, especially if you are feeling low, usually indicates the presence of your unicorn, who cares for you, thinks you are amazing and wants only your happiness. Be still, and if you don't already know its name, feel free to ask: it will probably pop into your mind. Thank it for helping you and lending you its strength, and invite it to stay with you. It will not say no.

Your unicorn may take the image you already have of it in your mind, or it may appear in a different form, but whatever it looks like, you're sure to recognise it. Its character will be right for you, a spirit to balance your own. Playful or gracious, affectionate or fierce, it will be your connection to the wider world, your guide to all the forces that keep the planet spinning. Your unicorn will never threaten you or ask you to do anything to harm yourself, or anyone or anything else. The enchanted bond between you will empower and guard you, and fill you with joy.

———

It's going to be a

RAINBOWS

and

UNICORNS

kind of day.

FORMS OF A UNICORN

Your unicorn can appear in any form it wants.

As beings from a higher dimension, unicorns are, strictly
speaking, neither male nor female. They can easily appear
as either, depending on the needs or wishes of their human,
and there's nothing to stop them appearing together in family
groups if they so desire and if it helps their human.

Whatever form your unicorn takes, it is always the fierce
protector of the pure-hearted and compassionate, the healer and
noble guardian of the natural world. As such, it may be awesome,
but it will never choose to be frightening. Our unicorns know
what we fear and will never do anything to upset us.

Here are some of the forms your unicorn might take
when it appears to you.

UNICORN

In much of Western art the unicorn, or *monoceros* – Greek for
'single horn' – is usually depicted as a small white horse with a
single, slender, straight horn projecting from between its eyes.
If your unicorn appears to you in this form, it may have a long,
flowing mane and tail, and a slightly more elegant form than
the average horse. Sometimes it can appear small and deer- or
goat-like, with cloven hooves, a delicate mane and a smooth
tail with a long tuft of hair at the end like a that of a lion.
This unicorn is trusting, affectionate and intelligent.

ALICORN

Today the word *alicorn* is used as a name for a winged unicorn.
This graceful creature is younger and less well-known than the
wingless one, but it is increasingly seen. Unicorns, as creatures
of pure energy, can 'fly' without wings – they move through
all earthly elements with ease – but the winged form adds an
element of contemplation and embodies the ability we all have
to rise above our problems to a higher plane of being. Alicorns
represent the power to change evil into good, and may bond
with people whose lives are especially difficult or harmful.

SEA UNICORN

Traditionally, the unicorn has a special relationship with water
– its horn purifies water of all poisons. Sea unicorns often
feature shimmering scales and manes and tails like sea-foam.
The sea unicorn's pedigree is very old, dating back to the time
of the Biblical flood. According to some legends, the unicorns
helped all the other animals to board Noah's Ark, leaving
themselves no time to get to safety. Yet the unicorns were so
special, so blessed, that they did not die, but rapidly evolved as
the flood washed over them, becoming narwhals, the unicorns
of the sea, who live to this day in cold Northern seas. Like the
narwhal, a sea unicorn may change colour as it grows, starting
out as blue-grey, then gently shading through blue-black in its
youth, to mottled grey as an adult and snowy white in old age.
Sea unicorns are selfless and giving.

FIRE UNICORN

These fierce unicorns have flaming manes and joyful, glittering
eyes. Like the Japanese *kirin*, the fire unicorn is considered to be
a very holy creature, only appearing in times of peace. It never
harms any other living thing, but if attacked will defend itself
fiercely, breathing fire from its nostrils. Some say its whole body
is covered with tiny flames. This unicorn brings good luck,
protection and success, and defends the good against evil.

WOODLAND UNICORN

Unicorns embody and protect the natural world, and often appear to us through its elements. Your unicorn might be made of flowers and leaves that dance with the arrival of spring. A shy creature, it might also signal its presence more discreetly, using the natural world to send a message just for you. Keep an eye out for little hints that your unicorn is with you. You may see a unicorn-shaped cloud above you, or catch a glimpse of its outline in a tree, a bush or a flower. Some say that the unicorn leaves a white feather to show it has passed, so if you see one floating on the wind or caught on a bush near you, and there are no white-feathered birds anywhere near, you may very well have been visited by one of these beautiful, magical creatures.

SKY UNICORN

Unicorns are creatures of moonlight and starlight.
A sky unicorn may appear as a cloud creature,
soft and dreaming, or filled with sparkling stars.
Its appearance can change with the phases of the
moon. The moon is most often regarded as female,
and this unicorn has a strong affinity for girls and
women rather than boys and men, possibly due
to its protective qualities. The sky unicorn is
a strong defender, always by your side.

Whatever form your unicorn takes, you will
come to recognise it for what it is and to welcome
the signs that remind you that your friend and
protector is near, guarding and guiding you.

Celebrating the sacred connection between the unicorn and the skies above is the constellation Monoceros.

It first appeared on a celestial globe in 1613, in the Northern sky between Orion the Hunter and Hydra the Watersnake. The beautiful Rosette Nebula marks this star unicorn's head, and the constellation also contains the faint but pretty Christmas Tree, Fox Fur and Cone Nebulas. Monoceros, in keeping with the unicorn's shy and secretive nature, is a very faint constellation, but it has blue eyes – a binary system of blue giant stars – and two planets orbit its golden heart star. Maybe these distant worlds are the original home of the unicorn!

When it rains, look for rainbows. **WHEN IT'S DARK, LOOK FOR STARS.**

HOW TO TALK TO YOUR UNICORN

By now, with a bit of perseverance and a fair wind, you
might already have met your very own unicorn. Perhaps,
while meditating, you might have experienced that
deep and sustaining sense of peace that is the hallmark
of a unicorn's presence. Perhaps you might have caught
a glimpse of your unicorn while you were dreaming.
Perhaps something as simple as a floating blossom might
have stood out to you with unusual clarity, and you
recognised in that a message just for you.

And maybe, just maybe, you have even reached out
and made contact.

Or, maybe, you aren't quite sure how to begin
communicating. After all, it's not every day that
you get the chance to address a unicorn for the
first time! And, though gentle, unicorns are
powerful, awe-inspiring creatures.

But you have nothing to fear. The unicorn has
an instinctive grasp of how to communicate
with other beings. And, more than anything,
it wants to communicate with *you*.

YOUR UNICORN'S NAME

Unicorns' names are unique and beautiful. Sometimes, they are associated with elements of the natural world – names such as Starlight, Sunlight, Moonglow, Ocean, Jasmine or Jewel all represent things that unicorns love. Quite often, unicorns take the names of precious stones, such as Diamond, Opal and Amethyst. Other unicorns may have unusual or foreign-sounding names that mean nothing to their humans but symbolise something deeply personal about the unicorns themselves. If you are particularly close to your unicorn, it might tell you what its name means, but this is a rare favour.

Very occasionally, your unicorn will allow you to choose a name to bestow upon it. It will let you know if this is the case. Usually, however, your unicorn will tell you its name itself, in dreams, in meditations or in the whisper of the wind.

However your unicorn chooses to share its name with you, value it. It is a gift – one whose power you might like to channel by using it as a mantra.

COMMUNICATING WITH UNICORNS

Unicorns are telepathic. Your unicorn may therefore speak
to you mind-to-mind in your native language. They
may also choose to communicate in other ways.
Yours may actually speak to you aloud.

Listen to what it says, but also memorise its voice: does it sound
melodious like chimes or gentle bells, or light like a breeze?
Can you hear a slight crackle of flames beneath the words? Or
is it more like flowing water, rain or ocean waves? Sometimes
your unicorn's voice will echo its visual appearance, but
sometimes it will contrast with it. If your unicorn came from
the sea, does its voice sound like waves, or fire? A powerful,
earthy unicorn may have a voice that makes you think of rolling
thunder among mountains – or starlight! There are no rules.

Your unicorn may also choose to share images with you telepathically, of places it has seen or strange animals that inhabit other dimensions. It may even let you see mental pictures of its home!

Not all unicorns use verbal language. Your unicorn may feel that empathising with your emotions – connecting with you directly at the level of feelings – is a better way for you both to communicate. If you're worried, your unicorn may seek to soothe you. If you're feeling low, it may fill you with happiness. If you're feeling unwell, it may look to heal you. Unicorns these days often focus on healing illnesses of the spirit, rather than the body – your unicorn's healing is less likely to come from powdered horn than the quiet but overpowering sense of its unwavering support.

Sometimes unicorns use body language, which can be a truly amazing thing. A slight tilt of the head, the waggle of an ear, a nod, a gentle touch of the horn to your shoulder – all loving reassurance to let you know your unicorn will always be there for you. Unicorns are musical creatures and this is one of the most powerful languages we share. There are few things that can fill you with more joy than watching your unicorn move in time to your favourite music, or hearing a hint of its silvery song.

If you
stumble,
make it
part
of the
dance.

TOTALLY IN TUNE

If you're very lucky, and your unicorn is feeling particularly loving, it may even let you ride it. This is *very* rare. Being invited to walk beside it, with one hand in its mane, is more likely, and a joy in itself. Try to capture the feel of the mane, whether it's warm or cool, silky or rough, light or heavy. Does it feel like trailing your hand in water, or dipping it in soft, powdery snow? Or does it feel like the wind through your fingers? Bring it to mind if you feel unsure of yourself in your day-to-day life. It will comfort and encourage you.

Sometimes you will find yourself simply, completely in tune with your unicorn, knowing what you both feel and sharing your inner selves, silently and freely. Such moments can inspire and empower you, and can even change your life.

WHAT YOU SEEK IS SEEKING YOU.

When you return to your day-to-day life, keep an eye out for signs that your unicorn is nearby, whether in nature or even in the heart of the city. Unicorns often appear as decorations on official buildings, or even sometimes on ordinary houses. All of these should reassure you that your friend and protector is guarding and guiding you.

A MAGICAL CONNECTION

You have now made contact with your unicorn – an incredible, life-changing experience. Now it will be there to help you any time you ask. Learning to strengthen and enhance your bond will only make it easier and more rewarding every time you call on your unicorn.

And you should call on your unicorn! Don't be shy about it. Meeting up with your unicorn at the same time every day (or week, or month) is a great way of setting aside time to deeply relax, recharge your batteries and de-stress. Your unicorn will enjoy this quality time it spends with you, too. There are a number of ways to fully engage in this incredible time and tools to help you focus your energies when you do. You should feel free to try different methods until you find the ones that work best for you.

In almost all cases, the first step is to get comfortable. So
go on, if you have something important to do, get it out
of the way first. It's best not to have any distractions.

Just like when you first sought your unicorn, it can help
to play relaxing music. Choose something you think your
unicorn might like and that it has responded to before.
Sit or lie somewhere restful. Wear loose, comfortable
clothing and make sure you aren't hungry or thirsty.

Now you're ready to use some of the tools at our disposal
to help us engage more deeply with unicorns.

AMAZING AMULETS

Many of us have something we wear or carry to bring
us luck. A small token that help us to feel safe. It may
be a piece of jewellery, or perhaps a particular article of
clothing. Whatever it is, it's something that means a lot to
us, something we don't like to be parted from, something
that often provides a physical link to a significant memory,
person or place that we treasure. This is an *amulet* or *charm*,
and it can be a powerful focus for your positive energies
when you summon your unicorn.

There are many unicorn amulets around, usually in the
form of pendants, rings or earrings. In your search for your
unicorn, you may have already been led to one that is perfect
for you. If so, you will have been able to tell – your unicorn
will let you know if the amulet that speaks to you is the right
one, whether it arrived as a present from someone or you
found it quite accidentally when you weren't looking for it.

Amulets can be very simple but beautiful. Or they can be something that only looks like a unicorn when seen from a certain angle or in certain lights. But you will know your amulet when you see it. Ask your unicorn for advice and be sure and confident in the choices you make.

Very wise and old unicorns are said to grow a gemstone at the place where their horn emerges from their head. This jewel is described as a ruby or carnelian, and contains all the unicorn's power. Anyone who finds one is especially lucky and blessed: legend has it that the gem dispels poison, prevents illness and chases away sadness and nightmares. Unsurprisingly, it makes an excellent amulet. Equally unsurprisingly, these gems are very rare! But you may find a red gemstone helps to invoke some of the unicorn's serenity and calm.

CRYSTAL CLEAR

There's a huge variety of crystals on and in the earth, from
the simplest (and cheapest) quartz to rare and expensive
gemstones, such as diamonds. And that's not including the
man-made or man-altered ones, like goldstone or rainbow
aura quartz. The crystals that you respond to can say a lot
about you. Are you as transparent, clear and serene as golden
citrine, or dark and mysterious as onyx? Eco-friendly and as
green as malachite, or as passionate and luxurious as ruby?
Hard as diamond, or tranquil as turquoise? Like most of us,
you may be all of them at different times.

Small crystals, polished or unpolished, are easy to find or buy
and make good meditation aids. Spheres and rutile quartz
(sometimes known as 'angel hair crystal') are ideal. When you
find the one that makes you think of your unicorn, be sure to
recognise your gratitude for the discovery, and treasure it.

TALISMANS

A talisman is something we make for ourselves, dedicating time, energy and willpower to creating it exactly the way we want it to be. If you feel the desire to create your own talisman, don't be too tough on yourself. It doesn't need to be perfect – your unicorn will love it anyway, because freeing your creativity will always bring you closer together. Together, you can share the joy of learning something new or gaining a skill.

If you like crafts, use your skills to make a unicorn figure, or paint a portrait of your unicorn. You can try making your own jewellery or accessories, or perhaps working the figure of your unicorn into a pottery project. If there is an art or craft you've always wanted to try, but not got around to yet, give it a go!